My United States

Arkansas

MARTIN GITLIN

Children's Press®
An Imprint of Scholastic Inc.

Content Consultant

James Wolfinger, PhD, Associate Dean and Professor
College of Education, DePaul University, Chicago, Illinois

Library of Congress Cataloging-in-Publication Data
Names: Gitlin, Marty, author.
Title: Arkansas / by Martin Gitlin.
Description: New York, NY : Children's Press, an imprint of Scholastic Inc., [2018] | Series: A true book | Includes
    bibliographical references and index.
Identifiers: LCCN 2017051024 | ISBN 9780531235560 (library binding) | ISBN 9780531250747 (pbk.)
Subjects: LCSH: Arkansas—Juvenile literature.
Classification: LCC F411.3 .G88 2018 | DDC 976.7—dc23
LC record available at https://lccn.loc.gov/2017051024

Photographs ©: cover: Carol Barrington/Aurora Photos; back cover bottom: IrinaK/Shutterstock; back cover ribbon: AliceLiddelle/Getty Images; 3 bottom: Archive PL/Alamy Images; 3 map: Jim McMahon/Mapman ®; 4 left: oksana2010/Shutterstock; 4 right: Olga Popova/Shutterstock; 5 top: Wesley Hitt/Getty Images; 5 bottom: WilleeCole Photography/Shutterstock; 6 bottom: Robert Mayne USA/Alamy Images; 7 top: Michele and Tom Grimm/Alamy Images; 7 center: Michael Snell/Alamy Images; 7 bottom: Courtesy Arkansas Department of Parks & Tourism; 8-9: Walter Meayers Edwards/National Geographic/Getty Images; 11: Terry Smith Images/Alamy Images; 12: US Army Photo/Alamy Images; 13: Mary Liz Austin/Alamy Images; 14: Marijn Heuts/NiS/Minden Pictures; 15: Warren_Price/Getty Images; 16-17: buburuzaproductons/Getty Images; 19: Mark Reinstein/Corbis/Getty Images; 20: Tigatelu/Dreamstime; 22 left: Atlaspix/Shutterstock; 22 right: Brothers Good/Shutterstock; 23 top left: Olga Popova/Shutterstock; 23 center right: oksana2010/Shutterstock; 23 top right: Daniel Prudek/Shutterstock; 23 center left: WilleeCole Photography/Shutterstock; 23 bottom right: John Cancalosi/Alamy Images; 23 bottom left: Coprid/Shutterstock; 24-25: Buyenlarge/Getty Images; 27: Caddos walk in their village of grass huts (colour litho), Kihn, William Langdon (1898-1957)/National Geographic Creative/Bridgeman Images; 29: duncan1890/Getty Images; 30 left: Caddos walk in their village of grass huts (colour litho), Kihn, William Langdon (1898-1957)/National Geographic Creative/Bridgeman Images; 30 right: Atlaspix/Shutterstock; 31 bottom: TIM CLARY/AFP/Getty Images; 31 top left: Buyenlarge/Getty Images; 31 top right: Bettmann/Getty Images; 32: Prestor Pictures LLC/Alamy Images; 33: Bettmann/Getty Images; 34-35: Wesley Hitt/Getty Images; 36: Chris Brashers/Icon Sportswire/Getty Images; 37: Education & Exploration 2/Alamy Images; 38: Bill Barksdale/Getty Images; 39: HittProductions/Getty Images; 40 inset: Joshua Resnick/Shutterstock; 40 background: PepitoPhotos/iStockphoto; 41: Wesley Hitt/Getty Images; 42 top: IanDagnall Computing/Alamy Images; 42 bottom left: Sporting News and Rogers Photo Archive/Getty Images; 42 center: Sporting News Archive/Getty Images; 42 bottom right: William N. Jacobellis/New York Post Archives/NYP Holdings, Inc./Getty Images; 43 top left: Santi Visalli/Getty Images; 43 top right: Ron Galella/Getty Images; 43 center left top: Michael Ochs Archives/Getty Images; 43 center right: Everett Collection Historical/Alamy Images; 43 center left bottom: INTERFOTO/Alamy Images; 43 bottom left: AF archive/Alamy Images; 43 bottom right: Greg Doherty/Getty Images; 44 top: Minden Pictures/Superstock, Inc.; 44 bottom left: Pine Bluff Commercial, Ralph Fitzgerald/AP Images; 44 bottom right: Caddos walk in their village of grass huts (colour litho), Kihn, William Langdon (1898-1957)/National Geographic Creative/Bridgeman Images; 45 top: Reinhard Eisele/Mauritius/Superstock, Inc.; 45 center: Marc F. Henning/Alamy Images; 45 bottom: Buyenlarge/Getty Images.

Maps by Map Hero, Inc.

Scholastic Inc., 557 Broadway, New York, NY 10012

1 2 3 4 5 6 7 8 9 10 R 28 27 26 25 24 23 22 21 20 19

Front cover: Buffalo National River

**Back cover: Frozen waterfall
at Glory Hole Falls**

Welcome to Arkansas

Find the Truth!

Everything you are about to read is true *except* for one of the sentences on this page.

Which one is **TRUE**?

T or F People from Arkansas fought on both sides of the Civil War.

T or F Several U.S. presidents were born in Arkansas.

UNITED STATES

Arkansas

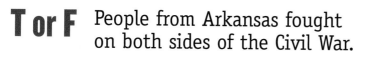

Arkansas
706 BSZ
The Natural State

Find the answers in this book.

3

Contents

THE **BIG** TRUTH!

Pecan

What Represents Arkansas?

Apple blossom

4

Buffalo National River

White-tailed deer fawn

This Is Arkansas!

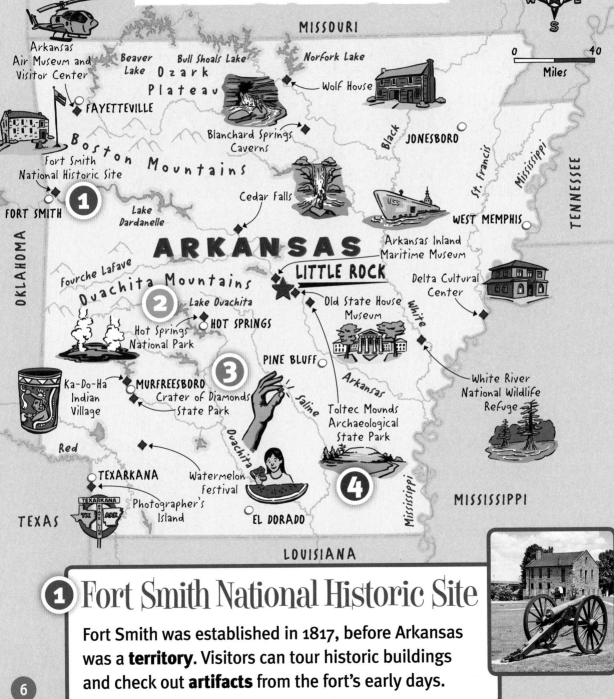

MISSOURI

Arkansas Air Museum and Visitor Center

Beaver Lake

Bull Shoals Lake

Norfork Lake

Wolf House

Ozark Plateau

FAYETTEVILLE

Blanchard Springs Caverns

JONESBORO

Black

Boston Mountains

Fort Smith National Historic Site

①

FORT SMITH

Lake Dardanelle

Cedar Falls

ARKANSAS

USS

WEST MEMPHIS

Arkansas Inland Maritime Museum

LITTLE ROCK

Old State House Museum

Delta Cultural Center

OKLAHOMA

Fourche Lafave

Ouachita Mountains

②

Lake Ouachita

Hot Springs National Park

HOT SPRINGS

White

PINE BLUFF

③

Arkansas

White River National Wildlife Refuge

Ka-Do-Ha Indian Village

MURFREESBORO

Crater of Diamonds State Park

Saline

Toltec Mounds Archaeological State Park

Red

④

Ouachita

TEXARKANA

Watermelon Festival

Photographer's Island

EL DORADO

Mississippi

MISSISSIPPI

TEXARKANA

TX   ARK

TEXAS

LOUISIANA

St. Francis

Mississippi

TENNESSEE

N
W   E
S

0   40
Miles

① Fort Smith National Historic Site

Fort Smith was established in 1817, before Arkansas was a **territory**. Visitors can tour historic buildings and check out **artifacts** from the fort's early days.

② Hot Springs National Park

At this national park, hot water from deep inside the earth rises up to form pools on the surface. Visitors can view these beautiful hot springs as they hike through the area. They can also soak in pools filled with hot water from the springs.

③ Crater of Diamonds State Park

This Murfreesboro site is the only place in the country where visitors can dig for diamonds and keep them. It is believed to have once been a volcano that brought diamonds to the earth's surface more than 100 million years ago.

④ Toltec Mounds Archaeological State Park

This site hosts three enormous earthen mounds built by the Woodland and Mississippian peoples sometime between 650 and 1050 CE. It is named for Mexico's Toltec people, who were once mistakenly thought to have built the mounds.

The Ozark Mountains are probably named after Aux Arc, a French trading post that was once located in the area.

CHAPTER 1

Land and Wildlife

Each year, when summer turns to fall, Arkansas is a wonderland of beauty. The plush greenery of evergreen trees atop the Ozark Mountains rises toward the white clouds above. Leaves of red, orange, green, and yellow adorn the trees below. Waterfalls flow into sparkling rivers, drawing bikers and hikers to explore the stunning scenery. Long stretches of flat grassland surround the water. Arkansans take pride in their home state's natural beauty. It is no wonder that Arkansas is nicknamed the Natural State.

Mountains, Fields, and Rivers

Arkansas's diverse landscape varies from region to region. The hilly Ozark Plateau of the north and Ouachita Mountains of the west contrast with the flat farmlands in the east. The many rivers of the state run mostly from northwest to southeast. They reach the Arkansas and Red Rivers and eventually the mighty Mississippi, which forms much of the state's eastern boundary.

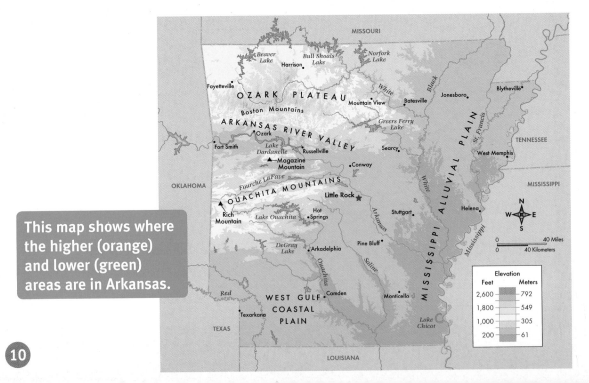

This map shows where the higher (orange) and lower (green) areas are in Arkansas.

Blanchard Springs Caverns

Located in the Ozark-St. Francis National Forests in north-central Arkansas, the Blanchard Springs Caverns were carved out by the flow of underground waters. Visitors can climb over rocks, slide down red clay mudslides, and get dirty as they explore the caves. The bright artificial lights in the caves also allow visitors to view the constantly changing **stalactites** and other rock formations inside. This is a great spot to explore underground!

No matter how hot or cold it is outside, it is always about 58 degrees Fahrenheit (14 degrees Celsius) inside Blanchard Springs Caverns.

What's the Temperature?

Temperatures in Arkansas are generally mild in the winter and hot in the summer. They range from 30 to 50 degrees Fahrenheit (–1 to 10 degrees Celsius) in January and 70° to 90°F (21° to 32°C) in July in the centrally located city of Little Rock.

The two highland regions in Arkansas bring distinctly different weather patterns. The Ouachita Mountains are in the state's wettest area, while the Ozarks are in the driest. Arkansas receives very little snow.

The town of Pocahontas flooded after record rainfall in 2017.

MAXIMUM TEMPERATURE
120°F

MINIMUM TEMPERATURE
-29°F

Growing Wild

About half of Arkansas is covered by forests. This means there is a huge variety of plant life in the state. Oak and hickory trees dominate the Ozarks area. These kinds of trees can also be found in a narrow, hilly area in the northeast called Crowley's Ridge. The hardwood forests of the Ouachita Mountains are filled with a number of pine species. The state's landscape has been changed by the creation of farmland. However, some of the original hardwood forests remain.

All Kinds of Animals

Deer, squirrels, and rabbits populate the fields and lakes of Arkansas. Bobcats seek food in the state's hills. Black bears can be seen in the Ozarks. The lakes and streams are packed with fish such as bass, walleye, and trout. Arkansas is also famous for the razorbacks that roam many parts of the state. These **feral** hogs were once domestic animals that later escaped or were released to be hunted.

Arkansas is home to about 300 bird species. Among them are bald eagles, hawks, barn owls, blue jays, and cardinals. Recent sightings of the rare ivory-billed woodpecker added to the large number of birds that are native to Arkansas.

Arkansas's location near the Mississippi River brings many **migratory** birds to the state. Ducks and geese can be seen stopping for food or flying through the skies as they make their journeys across the country.

Snow geese visit Arkansas each winter as part of their annual migration.

The Arkansas capitol measures about 213 feet (65 meters) high from the ground to the top of the dome.

CHAPTER 2

Government

Arkansas's capital, Little Rock, is easily the largest city in the state. Its population is more than double that of the state's second-largest city, Fort Smith. Little Rock was named the capital of the Arkansas Territory in 1821. It became the official state capital when Arkansas gained statehood in 1836. The city was named after a rock formation along the south bank of the Arkansas River. French explorer Jean-Baptiste Bénard de La Harpe called it *la petit roche*. This translates to "the little rock" in English.

Three Branches

The Arkansas government consists of three branches: executive, legislative, and judicial. The governor leads the executive branch and appoints a cabinet to run various state agencies. The legislative branch is called the Arkansas General Assembly. It consists of the House of Representatives and the Senate. The judicial branch includes the Arkansas Supreme Court and many smaller courts.

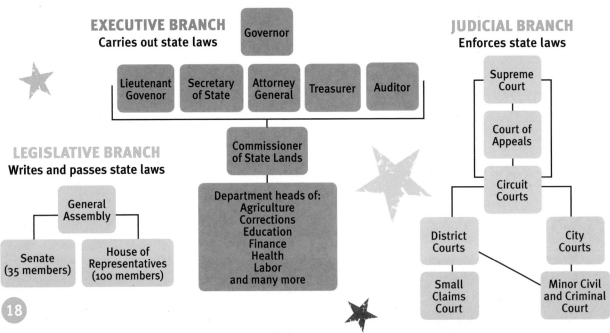

ARKANSAS'S STATE GOVERNMENT

EXECUTIVE BRANCH
Carries out state laws

Governor

Lieutenant Govenor | Secretary of State | Attorney General | Treasurer | Auditor

Commissioner of State Lands

Department heads of:
Agriculture
Corrections
Education
Finance
Health
Labor
and many more

LEGISLATIVE BRANCH
Writes and passes state laws

General Assembly

Senate (35 members) | House of Representatives (100 members)

JUDICIAL BRANCH
Enforces state laws

Supreme Court

Court of Appeals

Circuit Courts

District Courts | City Courts

Small Claims Court | Minor Civil and Criminal Court

Since leaving office in 2001, Bill Clinton has devoted himself to running the Clinton Foundation, a charitable organization that works to solve a wide variety of global issues.

Arkansas's Only President

So far, only one Arkansan has served as a U.S. president. Bill Clinton was born in Hope, Arkansas, near the borders of Texas and Oklahoma, in 1946. Since his youth, he always dreamed of being a politician. He started his career in office in 1976 when he was elected as the attorney general of Arkansas. Two years later, he ran for governor and won. In 1992, after years of successful leadership in Arkansas, he was elected president of the United States. He easily won reelection in 1996.

Arkansas in the National Government

Each state elects officials to represent it in the U.S. Congress. Like every state, Arkansas has two senators. The U.S. House of Representatives relies on a state's population to determine its numbers. Arkansas has four representatives in the House.

Every four years, states vote on the next U.S. president. Each state is granted a number of electoral votes based on its number of members in Congress. With two senators and four representatives, Arkansas has six electoral votes.

2 senators and 4 representatives

6 electoral votes

With six electoral votes, Arkansas's voice in presidential elections is below average compared to other states.

The People of Arkansas

Elected officials in Arkansas represent a population with a range of interests, lifestyles, and backgrounds.

Ethnicity (2016 estimates)

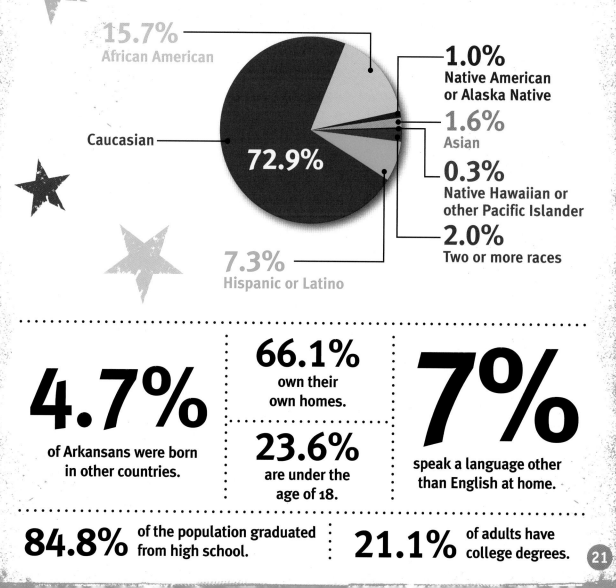

15.7%
African American

1.0%
Native American
or Alaska Native

1.6%
Asian

0.3%
Native Hawaiian or
other Pacific Islander

2.0%
Two or more races

Caucasian

72.9%

7.3%
Hispanic or Latino

4.7%
of Arkansans were born
in other countries.

66.1%
own their
own homes.

23.6%
are under the
age of 18.

7%
speak a language other
than English at home.

84.8% of the population graduated
from high school.

21.1% of adults have
college degrees.

What Represents Arkansas?

States choose specific animals, plants, and objects to represent the values and characteristics of the land and its people. Find out why these symbols were chosen to represent Arkansas or discover surprising curiosities about them.

Seal

An American bald eagle in the state seal is holding arrows in its claws to represent Arkansas's fighting spirit and an olive branch to represent peace. Beside the eagle are an angel and a sword symbolizing mercy and justice. Other symbols in the seal symbolize hard work and industry.

Flag

The Arkansas state flag was created in red, white, and blue to signify American pride. The U.S. flag boasts the same colors. The 25 white stars show that Arkansas was the 25th state to join the country. The diamond shape signifies that Arkansas is the only diamond-producing state.

Pecan

STATE NUT

About 1 million pounds (453,592 kilograms) of pecans are produced in Arkansas every year.

Honeybee

STATE INSECT

Honeybee pollination plays an important role in Arkansas agriculture.

Apple Blossom

STATE FLOWER

The town of Lincoln holds an annual apple festival.

White-Tailed Deer

STATE MAMMAL

This swift animal can run up to 40 miles (64 kilometers) per hour and jump 9-foot (3 m) fences.

Milk

STATE BEVERAGE

On average, each dairy cow in Arkansas produces about 3.7 gallons (14 liters) of milk per day.

Bauxite

STATE ROCK

Arkansas is rich in bauxite deposits, which produce the materials used to make soft drink cans and aluminum foil.

About 5,500 black Arkansans fought for the Union during the Civil War (1861-1865).

The Union defeated the Confederacy at the Battle of Pea Ridge in northwestern Arkansas during the Civil War.

CHAPTER 3

History

More than 450 years have passed since European explorers began arriving in what is now Arkansas. But human activity in the area began long before that. It is estimated that people have lived in Arkansas for at least 11,500 years. However, the area has never had a very large population. In 1810, after centuries of Native American settlement and European exploration, just 1,062 people lived in what is now Arkansas. However, Arkansas's population has continued to rise nearly every decade since, finally reaching a total of about 3 million today.

The First Arkansans

The Paleo-Indian, Archaic, Woodland, and Mississippian peoples were the earliest residents of Arkansas. Stone tools, animal bones, artwork, and other artifacts have provided clues about these early cultures. They created clay containers that remained intact for hundreds of years. They also painted pictures on cave walls and built huge mounds of earth throughout the state.

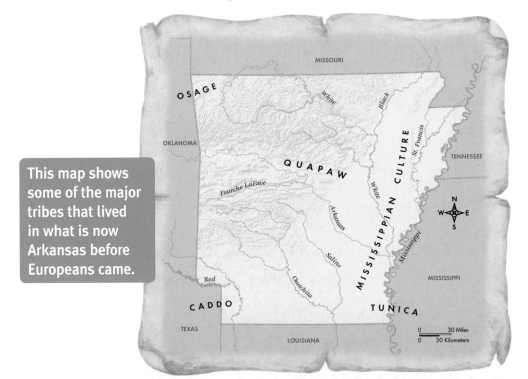

This map shows some of the major tribes that lived in what is now Arkansas before Europeans came.

The Caddo built sturdy, dome-shaped houses by covering wooden frames with dried grass.

A Land of Many Cultures

Over time, Arkansas's early inhabitants began settling down in different areas and developing into a wide range of cultures. By the 1500s, such groups as the Caddo, Quapaw, Osage, Mississippian, and Tunica were living in the mountains, valleys, and plains of the area that is now Arkansas. They built villages, towns, and farms. They had their own languages, art styles, and traditions. But their lives would soon be changed forever when European explorers came to the area.

New Arrivals

In 1541, Spanish explorer Hernando de Soto became the first European to visit Arkansas. De Soto and his men brought European diseases that the Native Americans were not used to. Huge numbers of people died as a result.

Europeans did not settle permanently in the area until the late 1600s, after France claimed the region. By then, due to disease and war, few Native Americans remained in the region.

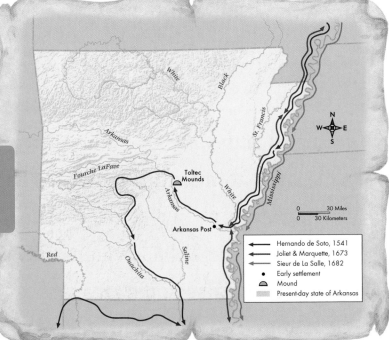

This map shows routes Europeans took as they explored and settled what is now Arkansas.

Growth Spurt

In 1803, the United States purchased all of present-day Arkansas as part of a larger land deal called the Louisiana Purchase. At the time, few white people lived there. But in 1819, the Arkansas Territory

Explorer René-Robert Cavelier, sieur de La Salle, claimed the land that is now Arkansas for France.

was officially established. Huge numbers of Americans began moving in. They started farms and began building homes and businesses. New towns and cities soon dotted the territory.

From Statehood to Secession

Arkansas Territory officials decided to pursue statehood in early 1836. They drew up the first state **constitution**, and the U.S. Congress admitted Arkansas as the nation's 25th state on June 15.

Rich slave owners controlled Arkansas's state government and businesses. As a result, the state **seceded** and joined the **Confederacy** in 1861, as the Civil War (1861–1865) was about to start.

Timeline of Arkansas Events

9500 BCE
Native Americans are living in what is now Arkansas.

1803
Arkansas becomes part of the United States as part of the Louisiana Purchase.

| 9500 BCE | 1541 CE | 1803 | 1836 |

1541 CE
Spaniard Hernando de Soto becomes the first European to explore modern-day Arkansas.

June 15, 1836
Arkansas becomes the 25th state.

Around 60,000 young Arkansans signed up to fight for the Confederacy when the war began. But some 14,000 Arkansans joined the Union army. The most significant clash in Arkansas was the Battle of Pea Ridge in March 1862. The Union victory forced the Confederates out of the state. As a result, Union soldiers were able to capture Little Rock the following year with little resistance.

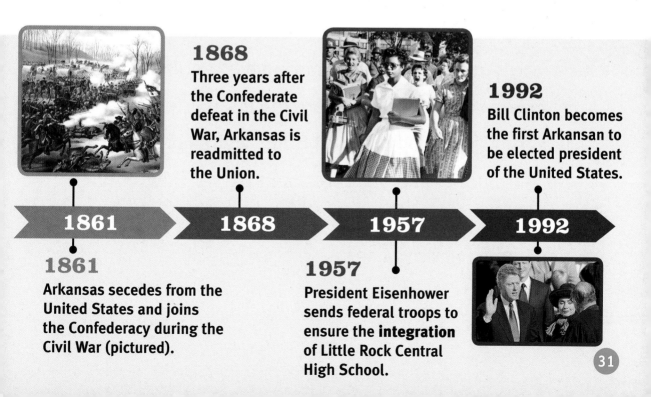

1868
Three years after the Confederate defeat in the Civil War, Arkansas is readmitted to the Union.

1992
Bill Clinton becomes the first Arkansan to be elected president of the United States.

1861

1868

1957

1992

1861
Arkansas secedes from the United States and joins the Confederacy during the Civil War (pictured).

1957
President Eisenhower sends federal troops to ensure the **integration** of Little Rock Central High School.

WARNING

NEGROS MUST STAY IN COLORED TOWN

"AFTER DARK"
UNLESS YOU ARE WORKING

Signs like this one were used to enforce segregation in the mid-20th century.

Slavery and Segregation

With the war's end, the Confederate states returned to the United States and slavery was **abolished**. But the racism of the South would not die. **Segregation** was the law of the land in Arkansas. African Americans were denied basic civil rights such as voting. They were forced to attend inferior schools and banned from "whites only" restaurants, swimming pools, and parks. They were also required to sit in separate railroad cars and in the back of buses.

The Little Rock Nine

In the 1950s, the civil rights movement made a major push to end segregation. Arkansas became the site of one of the biggest events of the movement when nine black students attempted to attend Little Rock Central High School in 1957. Arkansas governor Orval Faubus tried to prevent the students from entering the school. Angry white mobs formed, threatening and harassing the nine courageous students. President Dwight Eisenhower was forced to send federal troops to escort them inside. The nine were badly mistreated by racist classmates that year, but they refused to give up. For their brave actions, the students became forever known as the Little Rock Nine.

At the annual Fat Tire Festival, mountain bikers gather in the town of Eureka Springs for races and other events.

BASIN PARK HOTEL

CHAPTER 4

Culture

There is always plenty to do and see in Arkansas. Many people across the state love to attend a variety of sporting events and root for their favorite teams. Art and music are also popular. The Viewfinder Photography Exhibit in El Dorado displays photographs by Arkansans of all ages. Each Fourth of July, Little Rock's Pops on the River allows folks to enjoy fireworks set to the music of the Arkansas Symphony Orchestra.

Rooting for the Razorbacks

Arkansas boasts no major professional sports teams, but fans root hard for the University of Arkansas Razorbacks. The football team is especially popular. Arkansas is also the home of two minor league baseball teams. The Northwest Arkansas Naturals are based in Springdale, while the Arkansas Travelers play their home games in North Little Rock.

The Arkansas Razorbacks have had winning records most seasons and are often ranked among the top college teams in the country.

At the Ozark Folk Center in Mountain View, traditional folk music is celebrated with concerts, classes, and more.

Fun Festivals

Arkansas offers a wide range of festivals celebrating the state's local specialties. The Arkansas Folk Festival in Mountain View celebrates Arkansas culture with music and dancing. The Blossom Festival in Magnolia features a sidewalk art show and steak cook-off. The Jonquil Festival in Washington shows off the beautiful jonquil flowers that grow in the spring. Among the highlights of the Scottish Festival in Batesville is a drumming competition.

In 2017, Arkansas farmers harvested 1,104,000 acres (446,773 hectares) of rice.

Thriving Farms and Beyond

Agriculture is a big part of the Arkansas economy. The state ranks first in the country in rice production. It produces about half the rice grown in the United States. It also ranks among the top states in cotton production. Other major crops include peanuts and soybeans. Many people in cities work in such fields as education, health care, and manufacturing. Some hold retail jobs, while others work for the state government.

Go, Truckers, Go!

Many of the trucks that roll across America begin their journey in Arkansas. And many of the people behind the wheels of those trucks make Arkansas their home. The state boasts 22 major trucking companies.

About 85,000 Arkansans work in more than 80 of the centers where trucks receive and drop off their loads. And about one in five Arkansas workers is connected in some way to the transportation of goods.

In addition to major companies, Arkansas is home to thousands of much smaller trucking businesses.

Fantastic Food

Many unique foods are linked to Arkansas. Deep-fried pickles are one popular treat. A dessert called possum pie is served in restaurants and homes throughout the state. So is chocolate gravy, which is often poured atop biscuits. Locally grown fruits include peaches and watermelon.

★ Twice-Cooked Oven-Fried Chicken

Ask an adult to help you!

Hearty, home-cooked dishes like this are a staple of Arkansas cuisine.

Ingredients

6 pounds chicken pieces
1 teaspoon salt
1/4 teaspoon curry powder
2 teaspoons black pepper

1/2 cup white flour
1/4 cup whole wheat flour
1 tablespoon cornmeal
1 teaspoon dry mustard
Oil for frying

Directions

Soak the chicken in cold salted water for 1 hour. Remove and pat dry. Combine all the dry ingredients in a bag or bowl. Toss the chicken in this mixture and coat well. Pour about an inch of oil in a heavy pan. Fry the chicken for 10 minutes on each side. Place the fried chicken on a foil-lined baking sheet. Bake for 25 minutes at 350°F. Enjoy!

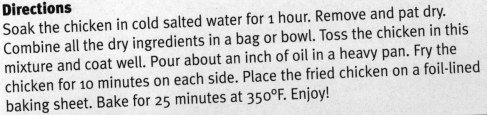

A kayaker enjoys the views along the Buffalo National River.

A Great State

Warm weather, stunning scenery, and a lot of water make Arkansas a wonderful state for outdoor fun. Lifelong Arkansans and visitors alike enjoy camping, boating, fishing, and hiking. But that's not all that draws people to this incredible state. Arkansas is also a place full of friendly people, fascinating history, and rich culture. There's truly something for everyone! ★

Famous People

Douglas MacArthur

(1880–1964) was a U.S. Army general whose strategies played a huge role in the defeat of Japan in World War II (1939–1945). He was born in Little Rock.

Florence Beatrice Price

(1887–1953) was born in Little Rock and became the first widely recognized African American classical composer. She also thrived as an organist, piano player, and teacher.

Dizzy Dean

(1910–1974) was among the greatest baseball pitchers of all time. Known as a colorful character, the Lucas native was voted into the Baseball Hall of Fame in 1953.

Bear Bryant

(1913–1983) is among the most successful college football coaches of all time. The Cleveland County native guided the Alabama Crimson Tide to six national championships in his 25 years as coach.

Daisy Bates

(1914–1999) was a prominent civil rights activist who led the campaign to integrate Little Rock Central High School in 1957. She also worked as a journalist and lecturer.

Helen Gurley Brown

(1922–2012) was best known as the editor in chief of *Cosmopolitan* magazine. The Green Forest native was a well-known author and publisher who came to fame in the early 1960s.

Johnny Cash

(1932–2003) was one of the most successful and influential country music singer-songwriters in history. He was born in Kingsland.

Glen Campbell

(1936–2017) was among the most famous and accomplished country music stars of his day. Born in Billstown, he performed such hits as "Wichita Lineman," "Galveston," and "Rhinestone Cowboy." He also hosted his own television variety show.

Al Green

(1946–) is a singer-songwriter and record producer whose hits included "Let's Stay Together" and "Love and Happiness." This Forrest City native was inducted into the Rock and Roll Hall of Fame in 1995.

Mary Steenburgen

(1953–) is a Newport native and Academy Award–winning actor who has starred in many films and television series.

Billy Bob Thornton

(1955–) is an actor and director who received two Academy Award nominations for his work in the film *Sling Blade*. The Hot Springs native is also a singer, songwriter, and musician.

John Grisham

(1955–) is among the most prolific and successful American authors ever. Born in Jonesboro, he is known for writing exciting thrillers about lawyers and court cases.

Did You Know That ...

More than 600,000 acres (242,811 ha) of lakes and nearly 10,000 miles (16,093 km) of streams and rivers can be found in Arkansas.

The World Championship Duck Calling Contest is held annually in Stuttgart. Here, duck hunters compete to see who can create the most realistic duck sounds.

The name Arkansas means "south wind" and is derived from the Native American word *akansa*. It was used to describe the Quapaw, a group that once inhabited the area.

The Ben Pearson Archery company in Pine Bluff was once the largest archery equipment company in the world. In the 1960s, it produced about 4,000 bows per day.

The first Walmart store opened in Rogers, Arkansas, in 1962. Today, there are thousands of Walmart stores around the world, but the company remains headquartered in Arkansas.

Did you find the truth?

T People from Arkansas fought on both sides of the Civil War.

F Several U.S. presidents were born in Arkansas.

Resources

Books

Bailer, Darice. *What's Great About Arkansas?* Minneapolis: Lerner Publications, 2014.

Poe, Marshall. *Little Rock Nine.* New York: Aladdin, 2008.

Prentzas, G. S. *Arkansas.* New York: Children's Press, 2015.

Rozett, Louise (ed.). *Fast Facts About the 50 States: Plus Puerto Rico and Washington, D.C.* New York: Children's Press, 2010.

Visit this Scholastic website for more information on Arkansas:
★ www.factsfornow.scholastic.com
Enter the keyword **Arkansas**

Important Words

abolished (uh-BAH-lisht) put an end to something officially

artifacts (AHR-tuh-fakts) objects made or changed by human beings, especially tools or weapons used in the past

Confederacy (kuhn-FED-ur-uh-see) the group of 11 states that declared independence from the rest of the United States just before the Civil War

constitution (kahn-stih-TOO-shuhn) the basic laws of a country or state that describe the rights of the people and the powers of the government

feral (FER-uhl) relating to or resembling a wild beast

integration (in-tih-GRAY-shuhn) the inclusion of people of all races

migratory (MYE-gruh-tor-ee) relating to animals or people that move from place to place on a regular basis

seceded (suh-SEED-id) formally withdrew from a group or an organization

segregation (seg-rih-GAY-shuhn) the act or practice of keeping people or groups apart

stalactites (stuh-LAK-tites) icicle-shaped mineral deposits that hang from the roof of a cave

territory (TER-ih-tor-ee) an area connected with or owned by a country that is outside the country's main borders

Index

Page numbers in **bold** indicate illustrations.

About the Author

Marty Gitlin is an educational book author based in Cleveland. He has had more than 120 books published since 2006. He won more than 45 awards as a newspaper journalist. Included was a first place for general excellence from the Associated Press. That organization also selected him as one of the top four feature writers in Ohio.